ABSITE STUDY PLAN FOR 99TH PERCENTILE

Yana Puckett, MD, MPH, MS

Table of Contents

1. Instructions
2. Study materials required
3. Daily study plan
   a. Esophagus
   b. Stomach
   c. Small Bowel
   d. Large Bowel
   e. The Liver
   f. Portal Hypertension
   g. Gallbladder
   h. Pancreas
   i. Spleen
   j. Hernia Surgery
   k. Endocrine
   l. Skin
   m. Thoracic
   n. Vascular Surgery
   o. Trauma
   p. Burn
   q. Critical Care

Instructions

1. This study plan is designed to get you prepared to take the ABSITE exam in 6 months and score very highly on it.

2. Each line represents the subject that needs to be reviewed in Cameron Current Surgical Therapy (12th Edition).

3. Fiser part 1 refers to The Absite Review by Steven Fiser first 1/2 of that chapter to be read 5 times and part 2, the second part of the chapter to be read 5 times.

4. The column next to each Cameron chapter is what you need to read/do questions in addition to reading that chapter that day.

5. On days where there is nothing in the second or third columns, two Cameron Chapters need to be read. However, if you can, this can be a break for you where you only need to

read just one chapter that day. Overall, try to read two

chapters on those days to give yourself extra days before the

test to memorize high yield material.

Resources that Need to be Purchased

1. Absitereview.com - Hardcover Review Manual and Attend at least one Review session.

2. SCORE Curriculum subscription (typically covered by your residency program). Questions only.

3. Truelearn.com (ABSITE Review Subscription)

4. New York General Surgery Board Review Videos Subscription

Books that Need to be Purchased

 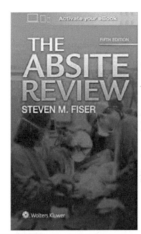  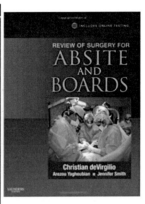

FISER Part 1

FISER Part 2

NY GEN SURG

SENIOR FISER

RED FISER

GREEN FISER

TRUELEARN

SCORE

ABSITEREVIEW

DE VIRGILIO

RUSH

SURGERY REVIEW ILLUSTRATED

Schedule

THE ESOPHAGUS

1. Esophageal Function Tests	**FISER Part 1**
2. The Management of Gastroesophageal Reflux Disease	**FISER Part 2**
3. New Approaches to Gastroesophageal Reflux Disease (LINX)	**SENIOR FISER**
4. The Management of Barrett's Esophagus	**RED FISER**
5. The Endoscopic Treatment of Barrett's Esophagus	**GREEN FISER**
6. The Management of Paraesophageal Hiatal Hernia	**SCORE**
7. The Management of Zenker's Diverticulum	**TRUELEARN**
8. The Management of Achalasia of the Esophagus	**NY GEN SURG**
9. The Management of Disorders of Esophageal Motility	**ABSITEREVIEW**
10. The Management of Esophageal Cancer	**DE VIRGILIO**
11. Neoadjuvant and Adjuvant Therapy of Esophageal Cancer	**RUSH**
12. The Use of Esophageal Stents	**SURGERY REVIEW ILLUSTRATED**
13. The Management of Esophageal Perforation	

THE STOMACH

14. The Management of Benign Gastric Ulcers	**FISER Part 1**	**NY GEN SURG**
15. The Management of Duodenal Ulcers	**FISER Part 2**	**ABSITEREVIEW**
16. The Management of the Zollinger-Ellison Syndrome	**SENIOR FISER**	**DE VIRGILIO**
17. The Management of the Mallory-Weiss Syndrome	**RED FISER**	**RUSH**
18. he Management of Gastric Adenocarcinoma	**GREEN FISER**	**SURGERY REVIEW ILLUSTRATED**
19. The Management of Gastrointestinal Stromal Tumors	**SCORE**	
20. The Management of Morbid Obesity	**TRUELEARN**	

THE SMALL BOWEL

21. Management of Small Bowel Obstruction	**FISER Part 1**	**ABSITEREVIEW**
22. The Management of Crohn's Disease of the Small Bowel	**FISER Part 2**	**DE VIRGILIO**
23. Strictureplasty in Crohn's Disease	**NY GEN SURG**	**RUSH**
24. The Management of Small Bowel Tumors	**SENIOR FISER**	**SURGERY REVIEW ILLUSTRATED**
25. The Management of Diverticulosis of the Small Bowel	**RED FISER**	
26. The Management of Motility Disorders of the Stomach and Small Bowel	**GREEN FISER**	
27. The Management of Short Bowel Syndrome	**TRUELEARN**	
28. The Management of Enterocutaneous Fistulas	**SCORE**	

29. *Preoperative Bowel Preparation Is It Necessary?*
30. *The Management of Diverticular Disease of the Colon*
31. *The Management of Chronic Ulcerative Colitis*
32. *The Management of Toxic Megacolon*
33. *The Management of Crohn's Colitis*
34. *The Management of Ischemic Colitis*
35. *The Management of Clostridium difficile Colitis*
36. *The Management of Large Bowel Obstruction*
37. *Enteral Stents in the Treatment of Colonic Obstruction*
38. *The Management of Acute Colonic Pseudo-Obstruction (Ogilvie's Syndrome)*
39. *The Management of Colonic Volvulus*
40. *The Management of Rectal Prolapse*
41. *The Management of Solitary Rectal Ulcer Syndrome*
42. *The Surgical Management of Constipation*
43. *The Management of Radiation Injury to the Small and Large Bowel*
44. *Surgery for the Polyposis Syndromes*
45. *The Management of Colon Cancer*
46. *The Management of Rectal Cancer*
47. *The Management of Tumors of the Anal Region*
48. *The Use of PET Scanning in the Management of Colorectal Cancer*
49. *Neoadjuvant and Adjuvant Therapy for Colorectal Cancer*
50. *The Management of Colonic Polyps*
51. *Management of Peritoneal Surface Malignancies of Appendiceal or Colorectal Origin*
52. *The Management of Acute Appendicitis*
53. *The Management of Hemorrhoids*
54. *The Management of Anal Fissures*
55. *The Management of Anorectal Abscess and Fistula*
56. *The Management of Anorectal Stricture*
57. *The Management of Pruritus Ani*
58. *Surgical Management of Fecal Incontinence*
59. *The Management of Rectovaginal Fistula*
60. *The Management of Anal Condyloma*
61. *The Management of Pilonidal Disease*

FISER Part 1

FISER Part 2

NY GEN SURG

SENIOR FISER

RED FISER

GREEN FISER

TRUELEARN

SCORE

ABSITEREVIEW

DE VIRGILIO

RUSH

SURGERY REVIEW ILLUSTRATED

62. The Management of Lower Gastrointestinal Bleeding
63. Enhanced Recovery After Surgery Colon Surgery

THE LIVER

1. The Management of Cystic Disease of the Liver	**FISER Part 1**
2. The Management of Echinococcal Cyst Disease of the Liver	**FISER Part 2**
3. The Management of Liver Hemangioma	**NY GEN SURG**
4. The Management of Benign Liver Lesions	**SENIOR FISER**
5. The Management of Malignant Liver Tumors	**RED FISER**
6. Hepatic Malignancy Resection Versus Transplantation	**GREEN FISER**
7. Ablation of Colorectal Carcinoma Liver Metastases	**TRUELEARN**
8. The Management of Hepatic Abscess	**SCORE**
9. Transarterial Chemoembolization for Liver Metastases	**ABSITEREVIEW**
10. Portal Hypertension and the Role of Shunting Procedures	**DE VIRGILIO**
11. Liver Transplantation	**RUSH**

12. Endoscopic Therapy for Esophageal Variceal Hemorrhage
13. Transjugular Intrahepatic Portosystemic Shunt
14. The Management of Refractory Ascites
15. The Management of Hepatic Encephalopathy
16. The Management of Budd-Chiari Syndrome

SURGERY REVIEW ILLUSTRATED

THE GALLBLADDER

1. The Management of Asymptomatic (Silent) Gallstones	**FISER Part 1**
2. The Management of Acute Cholecystitis	**FISER Part 2**
3. Management of Common Bile Duct Stones	**NY GEN SURG**
4. Laparoscopic Common Bile Duct Exploration	**SENIOR FISER**
5. The Management of Acute Cholangitis	**RED FISER**
6. The Management of Benign Biliary Strictures	**GREEN FISER**
7. The Management of Cystic Disorders of the Bile Ducts	**TRUELEARN**
8. The Management of Primary Sclerosing Cholangitis	**SCORE**
9. The Management of Bile Duct Cancer	**ABSITEREVIEW**
10. The Management of Gallbladder Cancer	**DE VIRGILIO**
11. The Management of Gallstone Ileus	**RUSH**
12. Transhepatic Interventions for Obstructive Jaundice	**SURGERY REVIEW ILLUSTRATED**

13. The Management of Acute Pancreatitis	**FISER Part 1**
14. The Management of Gallstone Pancreatitis, Part A	**FISER Part 2**
15. The Management of Gallstone Pancreatitis, Part B	**NY GEN SURG**
16. Pancreas Divisum and Other Variants of Dominant Dorsal Duct Anatomy	**SENIOR FISER**
17. The Management of Pancreatic Necrosis	**RED FISER**
18. The Management of Pancreatic Pseudocyst	**GREEN FISER**
19. Pancreatic Ductal Disruptions Leading to Pancreatic Fistula	**TRUELEARN**
20. Pancreatic Ascites, or Pancreatic Pleural Effusion	**SCORE**
21. The Management of Chronic Pancreatitis	**ABSITEREVIEW**
22. The Management of Periampullary Cancer	**DE VIRGILIO**
23. Vascular Reconstruction During the Whipple Procedure	**RUSH**
24. Palliative Therapy for Pancreatic Cancer	**SURGERY REVIEW ILLUSTRATED**
25. Neoadjuvant and Adjuvant Therapy for Localized Pancreatic Cancer	
26. Unusual Pancreatic Tumors	
27. Intraductal Papillary Mucinous Neoplasms of the Pancreas	
28. The Management of Pancreatic Islet Cell Tumors Excluding Gastrinomas	
29. Transplantation of the Pancreas	
30. Islet Allotransplantation for Diabetes	
31. Total Pancreatectomy and Autologous Islet Transplantation for Chronic Pancreatitis	

THE SPLEEN

1. Splenectomy for Hematologic Disorders	**FISER Part 1**	**SENIOR FISER**	**TRUELEARN**	**DE VIRGILIO**
2. The Management of Cysts, Tumors, and Abscesses of the Spleen	**FISER Part 2**	**RED FISER**	**SCORE**	**RUSH**
3. Splenic Salvage Procedures	**NY GEN SURG**	**GREEN FISER**	**ABSITEREVIEW**	**SURGERY REVIEW ILLUSTRATED**

HERNIA SURGERY

4. *The Management of Inguinal Hernia*	**FISER Part 1**	**TRUELEARN**
5. *The Management of Recurrent Inguinal Hernia Incisional, Epigastric, and Umbilical Hernias*	**FISER Part 2**	**SCORE**
6. *The Management of Semilunar, Lumbar, and Obturator Hernias*	**NY GEN SURG**	**ABSITEREVIEW**
7. *Core Muscle Injuries (Athletic Pubalgia, Sports Hernia)*	**SENIOR FISER**	**DE VIRGILIO**
8. *Abdominal Wall Reconstruction*	**RED FISER**	**RUSH**
9. *The Management of Benign Breast Disease*	**GREEN FISER**	**SURGERY REVIEW ILLUSTRATED**

10. Screening for Breast Cancer	**FISER Part 1**
11. The Role of Stereotactic Breast Biopsy in the Management of Breast Disease	**FISER Part 2**
12. Molecular Targets in Breast Cancer	**NY GEN SURG**
13. Breast Cancer Surgical Therapy	**SENIOR FISER**
14. Ablative Techniques in the Treatment of Benign and Malignant Breast Disease	**RED FISER**
15. Lymphatic Mapping and Sentinel Lymphadenectomy	**GREEN FISER**
16. The Management of the Axilla in Breast Cancer	**TRUELEARN**
17. Inflammatory Breast Cancer	**SCORE**
18. Ductal and Lobular Carcinoma in Situ of the Breast	**ABSITEREVIEW**
19. Advances in Neoadjuvant and Adjuvant Therapy for Breast Cancer	**DE VIRGILIO**
20. The Management of Recurrent and Metastatic Breast Cancer	**RUSH**
21. The Management of Male Breast Cancer	**SURGERY REVIEW ILLUSTRATED**
22. Breast Imaging Genetic Counseling and Testing	
23. Contralateral Prophylactic Mastectomy	
24. Margins How to and How Big?	
25. Intraoperative Radiation for Breast Cancer	
26. Breast Reconstruction After Breast Cancer Treatment Goals, Options, and Reasoning	

ENDOCRINE

1. Adrenal Incidentaloma	**FISER Part 1**
2. The Management of Adrenal Cortical Tumors	**FISER Part 2**
3. The Management of Pheochromocytoma	**NY GEN SURG**
4. The Management of Thyroid Nodules	**SENIOR FISER**
5. Nontoxic Goiter	**RED FISER**
6. The Management of Thyroiditis	**GREEN FISER**
7. Hyperthyroidism	**TRUELEARN**
8. Surgical Approach to Thyroid Cancer	**SCORE**
9. Primary Hyperparathyroidism	**ABSITEREVIEW**
10. Evaluation and Management of Persistent or Recurrent Hyperparathyroidism	**DE VIRGILIO**
11. Secondary and Tertiary Hyperparathyroidism	**RUSH**
12. Metabolic Changes Following Bariatric Surgery	**SURGERY REVIEW ILLUSTRATED**
13. Glycemic Control and Cardiovascular Disease Risk Reduction After Bariatric Surgery	

SKIN

14. Nonmelanoma Skin Cancers	**FISER Part 1**	**ABSITEREVIEW**
15. The Management of Cutaneous Melanoma	**FISER Part 2**	**DE VIRGILIO**
16. The Management of Soft Tissue Sarcoma	**NY GEN SURG**	**RUSH**
17. Management of the Solitary Neck Mass	**SENIOR FISER**	**SURGERY REVIEW ILLUSTRATED**
18. Hand Infections	**RED FISER**	
19. Nerve Injury and Repair	**GREEN FISER**	
20. Extremity Gas Gangrene	**TRUELEARN**	
21. Necrotizing Skin and Soft Tissue Infections	**SCORE**	

THORACIC

22. The Management of Primary Chest Wall Tumors	**FISER Part 1**	**TRUELEARN**
23. Mediastinal Masses	**FISER Part 2**	**SCORE**
24. Primary Tumors of the Thymus	**NY GEN SURG**	**ABSITEREVIEW**
25. The Management of Tracheal Stenosis	**SENIOR FISER**	**DE VIRGILIO**
26. The Management of Acquired Esophageal Respiratory Tract Fistula	**RED FISER**	**RUSH**
27. Congenital Chest Wall Deformities	**GREEN FISER**	**SURGERY REVIEW ILLUSTRATED**

VASCULAR SURGERY

28. Open Repair of Abdominal Aortic Aneurysms

29. Endovascular Treatment of Abdominal Aortic Aneurysm

30. The Management of Ruptured Abdominal Aortic Aneurysm

31. Abdominal Aortic Aneurysm and Unexpected Abdominal Pathology

32. The Management of Thoracic and Thoracoabdominal Aortic Aneurysms

33. The Management of Acute Aortic Dissections

34. Carotid Endarterectomy

35. The Management of Recurrent Carotid Artery Stenosis

36. Balloon Angioplasty and Stents in Carotid Artery Occlusive Disease

37. The Management of Extracranial Carotid and Vertebral Artery Aneurysms

38. Brachiocephalic Reconstruction

39. Upper Extremity Arterial Occlusive Disease

40. Aortoiliac Occlusive Disease

41. Femoropopliteal Occlusive Disease

42. Tibioperoneal Arterial Occlusive Disease

43. Profunda Femoris Reconstruction

44. Femoral and Popliteal Artery Aneurysms

45. The Treatment of Claudication

46. Pseudoaneurysms and Arteriovenous Fistulas

47. Axillobifemoral Bypass Grafting in the Twenty-First Century

48. Peripheral Arterial Embolism

49. Acute Peripheral Arterial and Bypass Graft Occlusion

50. Thrombolytic Therapy

51. Atherosclerotic Renal Artery Stenosis

52. Raynaud's Phenomenon

53. Thoracic Outlet Syndrome

54. The Diabetic Foot

55. Gangrene of the Foot

56. Buerger's Disease (Thromboangiitis Obliterans)

57. Acute Mesenteric Ischemia

58. The Management of Chronic Mesenteric Ischemia

FISER Part 1

FISER Part 2

NY GEN SURG

SENIOR FISER

RED FISER

GREEN FISER

TRUELEARN

SCORE

ABSITEREVIEW

DE VIRGILIO

RUSH

SURGERY REVIEW ILLUSTRATED

59. Hemodialysis Access Surgery

60. Venous Thromboembolism Prevention, Diagnosis,
and Treatment

61. Vena Cava Filters

62. Lymphedema

63. The Management of Lower Extremity Amputations

TRAUMA

1. Initial Assessment and Resuscitation of the Trauma Patient	**FISER Part 1**
2. Prehospital Management of the Trauma Patient	**FISER Part 2**
3. Airway Management in the Trauma Patient	**NY GEN SURG**
4. The Surgeon's Use of Ultrasound in Thoracoabdominal Trauma	**SENIOR FISER**
5. Emergency Department Thoracotomy	**RED FISER**
6. The Management of Traumatic Brain Injury	**GREEN FISER**
7. Chest Wall, Pneumothorax, and Hemothorax	**TRUELEARN**
8. Blunt Abdominal Trauma	**SCORE**
9. Penetrating Abdominal Trauma	**ABSITEREVIEW**
10. The Management of Diaphragmatic Injuries	**DE VIRGILIO**
11. The Management of Liver Injuries	**RUSH**
12. Pancreatic and Duodenal Injuries	**SURGERY REVIEW ILLUSTRATED**
13. Injuries to the Small and Large Bowel	
14. The Management of Rectal Injuries	
15. Injury to the Spleen	
16. Retroperitoneal Injuries	
17. Kidney and Ureter Damage Control Operation	
18. Urologic Complications of Pelvic Fracture	
19. Spine and Spinal Cord Injuries	
20. Evaluation and Management of the Patient With Craniomaxillofacial Trauma	
21. Penetrating Neck Trauma	
22. Blunt Cardiac Injury	
23. Abdominal Compartment Syndrome and Management of the Open Abdomen	
24. Blood Transfusion Therapy in Trauma	
25. Coagulation Issues and the Trauma Patient	
26. The Abdomen That Will Not Close	
27. The Management of Vascular Injuries	
28. Endovascular Management of Arterial Injury	
29. The Management of Extremity Compartment Syndrome	

BURN

	FISER Part 1	SENIOR FISER	TRUELEARN	DE VIRGILIO
1. Burn Wound Management				
2. Medical Management of the Burn Patient	FISER Part 2	RED FISER	SCORE	RUSH
3. The Management of Frostbite, Hypothermia, and Cold Injuries Electrical and Lightning Injury	NY GEN SURG	GREEN FISER	ABSITEREVIEW	SURGERY REVIEW ILLUSTRATED

4. Fluid and Electrolyte Therapy
5. Frailty and the Surgical Care of the Older Adult
6. Preoperative Preparation of the Surgical Patient
7. Is a Nasogastric Tube Necessary After Alimentary Tract Surgery?
8. Surgical Site Infections
9. The Management of Intra-Abdominal Infections
10. Occupational Exposure to Human Immunodeficiency Virus and Other Bloodborne Pathogens
11. Antifungal Therapy in the Surgical Patient
12. Measuring Outcomes of Surgery
13. Comparative Effectiveness Research in Surgery
14. Surgical Palliative Care
15. Cardiovascular Pharmacology

16. Glucose Control in the Postoperative Period
17. Postoperative Respiratory Failure
18. Ventilator-Associated Pneumonia
19. Extracorporeal Life Support for Respiratory Failure
20. Tracheostomy, Part One
21. Tracheostomy, Part Two
22. Acute Kidney Injury in the Injured and Critically Ill
23. Electrolyte Disorders
24. Acid-Base Problems
25. Catheter Sepsis in the Intensive Care Unit
26. The Septic Response and Management Multiple Organ Dysfunction Syndrome
27. Multiple Organ Dysfunction and Failure Antibiotics for Critically Ill Patients
28. Endocrine Changes in Critical Illness
29. Nutrition Therapy in Critical Illness
30. Coagulopathy in the Critically Ill Patient

FISER Part 1
FISER Part 2
NY GEN SURG
SENIOR FISER

RED FISER
GREEN FISER
TRUELEARN

SCORE
ABSITEREVIEW
DE VIRGILIO
RUSH
SURGERY REVIEW ILLUSTRATED

Made in the USA
Middletown, DE
12 March 2018